A-6 INTRUDER
CARRIER-BORNE BOMBER

Cover illustrations: front, an A-6E Intruder of VA-145 'Swordsmen' in the Pacific (see illustration D); back top, an A-6E aboard USS *Coral Sea* in 1986 (see illustration F); back bottom, an A-6E of the VA-42 'Green Pawns' (see illustration 54).

1. An Intruder for all ages. The blunt nose, high wings, high angle of attack and stalky landing gear are timeless characteristics of an attack bomber that has carried the night- and all-weather burden for the American Fleet since the mid-1960s. This black-nosed A-6A Intruder settling for a landing with unique wingtip flaps extended belongs to the 'Black Falcons' of VA-85, who have painted the squadron nickname on their wing-tanks. [*US Navy*]

A-6
INTRUDER
CARRIER-BORNE BOMBER

ROBERT F. DORR

ARMS AND
ARMOUR

*For
David
Anderton*

Arms and Armour Press
A Cassell Imprint
Villiers House. 41–47 Strand, London WC2N 5JE.

Distributed in the USA by Sterling Publishing Co. Inc.,
387 Park Avenue South, New York, NY 10016–8810.

Distributed in Australia by Capricorn Link (Australia)
Pty. Ltd, P.O. Box 665, Lane Cove, New South Wales
2066.

British Library Cataloguing in Publication Data
Dorr, Robert F.
A-6 Intruder carrier-borne bomber
I. Grumman A-6 aeroplanes
I. Title
623.7463
ISBN 1-85409-003-8

Designed and edited by DAG Publications Ltd.
Designed by David Gibbons; edited by David Dorrell;
layout by Anthony A. Evans; typeset by Ronset
Typesetters Ltd, Darwen, Lancashire; camerawork by
M&E Reproductions, North Fambridge, Essex;
printed and bound in Great Britain by The Alden
Press, Oxford.

G-59100

2. The original idea. When Lawrence M. (Larry) Mead and his Grumman design team began work on a future attack aircraft in the late 1950s, they had only a vague set of requirements to work with and were free to use imagination. The earliest design for what became the A-6 Intruder was an M-winged aircraft, seen here in model form in about 1958. While the wing and engine configurations were later changed completely, the model has side-by-side crew seating not very different from that of the real Intruder which followed. [*Grumman*]

3. Once the M-shaped wing was discarded and the Intruder became a more conventional swept-wing aircraft, Grumman built and displayed a full-scale mock-up at its Bethpage, Long Island, facility. The A2F-1 Intruder mock-up, seen here in 1959, was remarkably similar in appearance to the eventual aircraft. Curiously, the Corvus missile (not shown), which was to have been the new machine's primary ordnance, was cancelled at an early date, yet the Intruder became very effective carrying other kinds of ordnance. [*Grumman*]

NAVY

INTRODUCTION

When test pilot Robert Smyth took the Grumman Intruder on its maiden flight on 19 April 1960, he was flying an aircraft which looked, to many, like a holdover from the past rather than the wave of the future. The Intruder was slow. It was shaped like a tadpole. Fighter pilots joked that the blueprints had been reversed: the pointed end was not at the front. Other jet warplanes, notably the F-4 Phantom, busily amassed speed and altitude records in the early 1960s, while the Intruder could not even nudge through the sound barrier.

All it could do was carry a lot of bombs and deliver them with painstaking accuracy.

In the three decades since its first flight, the Grumman A-6 Intruder has confounded its critics and altered warfare. Part of the reason is the man in the right-hand seat, the only flight crewman in American uniform called a bombardier-navigator — or BN. Using the 'black box' gadgetry of a navigation bombing system called DIANE (digital integrated attack and navigation equipment), pilot and BN can take the Intruder against a target in the dead of night and the worst of weather. The epoch-making significance of the Intruder: it can hit that target with exquisite precision with neither crew member ever seeing it.

DIANE was not always a lady, and when VA-75 'Sunday Punchers' introduced the Intruder to Vietnam in 1965, equipment problems were endemic. But by 1966 (and with due respect to the USAF's 'Ryans Raiders' in their F-105Fs), the Intruder was the only warplane that could strike targets in North Vietnam at night in bad weather. A-6B and A-6C variants were created for special uses. The KA-6D tanker performed a different but vital role. In recent years, the A-6E TRAM Intruder (target recognition and attack, multi-sensor) proved itself in combat in the Lebanon and Libya, and against Iranian vessels in the Persian Gulf. During the Reagan years, the Intruder community flourished because Secretary of the Navy John Lehmann, a Naval Reserve A-6E BN, was a vocal proponent of the aircraft. The re-engined, redesigned A-6F Intruder of 1988 was one of the finest attack aircraft in the world. For a time it seemed that the A-6F would dominate carrier warfare in the 1990s and into the new century.

Instead, the US Navy has decided to leapfrog the A-6F (and the more modest, short-lived A-6G, which never flew) and to equip its future medium attack squadrons with the General Dynamics A-12A Avenger II. Production of the A-6F was cancelled, abruptly, in an election year (1988). The hi-tech, semi-'stealth' A-12A may prove to be as much a quantum leap as the Intruder was. Intruder crews will want to be convinced.

On the pages which follow, the reader will be able to look at the career of the Intruder from its inception to the present day. The author is responsible for any errors in this volume, but many others deserve credit.

This volume is dedicated to David Anderton, who taught most of us most of what we know, and who was a fixture with Grumman's *Horizons* magazine. The Grumman History Centre's Lois Lovisolo and Peter Kirkup helped greatly with research, expertise, and illustrations. I would also like to express my gratitude to Roger F. Besecker, John Dunnell, Rod Dymott, Jerry Geer, Clyde Gerdes, Roland P. Gill, Joseph G. Handelman DDS, William E. Johnson, Duane A. Kasulka, Robert L. Lawson, Frank R. MacSorley, Jim Sullivan and Chris Westhorp.

Robert F. Dorr
Oakton, Virginia

4

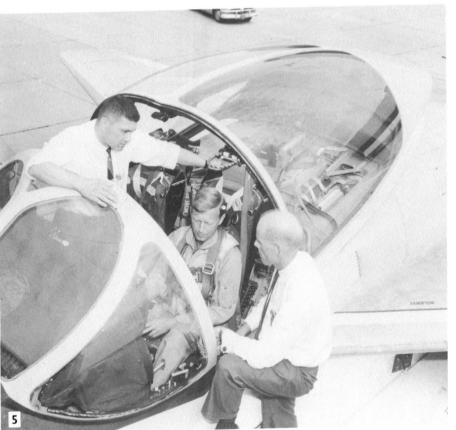

5

4. Shaped like a tadpole, the prototype Grumman A2F-1 Intruder makes its maiden flight at Long Island on 19 April 1960. On the first trip aloft in the new aircraft, test pilot Robert Smyth flew over the manufacturer's facilities at Calverton and Bethpage, delighting workers who helped produce the Intruder. Smyth later became an executive with Gulfstream Industries, while the Number One aeroplane, bureau number 147864, was employed in spin tests for the type. [*Grumman*]

5. The three most important figures in the early stages of the A2F-1 Intruder programme were Bruce Tuttle (left), head of the programme, test pilot Bob Smyth, and design team chief Lawrence M. (Larry) Mead. [*Grumman*]

6. Early in the Intruder flight development programme, Grumman posed this revealing view of an A-6A (formerly A2F-1) Intruder surrounded by examples of the ordnance it can carry. Some of the items, such as the AIM-9 Sidewinder missiles arranged in a quartet in front of the starboard wing, are seldom if ever carried in actual operations. [USN]

7. As soon as it had six Intruders that could be made airworthy at the same time, the US Navy staged this remarkable fly-by to demonstrate various weapons loads from Zuni rockets (foreground) to 500lb (227kg) bombs (fourth aircraft). Black radomes are typical of early Intruders. On 1 October 1962 the US designation system was changed and the A2F became the A-6. The A2F-1 Intruder model shown here became the A-6A. [Grumman]

8. The flight test programme for the A-6A Intruder was intense and ambitious. Generally it went well, and early tests confirmed the suitability of the Intruder as the Fleet's next medium attack aircraft. There was the occasional hitch, as happened to aircraft No 6 (bureau number 148616) which suffered a nose gear collapse. The 1961 mishap was especially damaging to the black radome which has been shattered and has begun to delaminate. But the aircraft was flying again soon afterwards. [Grumman]

6

7

8

9. The very first Intruder built and flown (bureau number 147963) was modified for spin tests with a parachute mounted in the cylindrical fairing at the tail for this somewhat hazardous type of manoeuvre. The prototype Intruder, seen here on 11 July 1962, also demonstrates the wingtip speed brakes which in due course replaced all fuselage-mounted speed brakes on Intruders. [*Grumman*]

10. Once the US Navy was pretty sure about the A-6A Intruder, it became time to test the warplane in the environment where it would be expected to fly and fight — aboard an aircraft-carrier. The eighth pre-production Intruder (bureau number 148618) is hoisted aboard the nuclear-powered USS *Enterprise* (CVAN-65) in December 1962 to begin the type's 'carquals', or carrier qualification trials. [*Grumman*]

11. At the time of the A-6A Intruder's carrier qualification trials, *Enterprise* was a new carrier, its nuclear power still new to the surface Navy, which had operated atomic-powered submarines for years. A carrier air wing had still to be embarked, which may explain the relatively pristine look of the flight deck in December 1962 as A-6A Intruder No 8 makes a perfect landing, catching the 'three wire' with its tailhook. From the beginning, there were problems with the Intruder's radar and electronics systems, but no difficulty was encountered which would prevent the type from serving at sea. [*Grumman*]

12. The dark rectangle below and ahead of the national insignia is the fuselage dive brake, which performed poorly and was eventually replaced by wingtip speed brakes. By the time Intruder No 10 (bureau number 149476) was depicted in this clean ground view, the shape of the vertical tail had been altered, creating a backward cant to the trailing edge of the fin. The overall shape of the Intruder – joked about by fighter pilots, who insisted that the pointed end should be at the front – was now destined to change little throughout the type's entire production run. [*Grumman*]

11

12

13. Six inches forward of the bombardier-navigator in the Intruder's left-hand seat, the pilot of the Navy's standard medium attack aircraft has plenty of space to work in, as well as excellent visibility. This 10 November 1986 view of an Intruder pilot also shows his helmet adorned with a silhouette of squadron VA-35's namesake, a Black Panther. [*USN*]

14. Early in the Intruder's production run, the US Marine Corps introduced the EA-6A Intruder, distinguished by the sizeable fairing atop its vertical fin and used for electronic warfare operations. The dark setting of this view of aircraft 156991 illustrates the Intruder's night- and all-weather capability. 'Bunnies' of Composite Squadron VMCJ-2, MCAS Cherry Point, North Carolina, adopted their emblem from *Playboy* magazine and emblazoned it on the EA-6A's tail. [*USMC*]

15. While the Intruder was being developed, aircraft No 4 was employed on bomb-carrying trials and was seen with a weapons load described by one naval officer as 'homongous', meaning awesome. In this posed view, the Intruder carries no fewer than thirty 500lb (227kg) bombs under four wing stations plus the fuselage centre-line. [*Grumman*]

16. The A-6B was a specialized version of the Intruder conceived for 'Iron Hand' suppression missions against SAM (surface-to-air missile) sites, and was armed with the AGM-78A Standard ARM (anti-radiation missile) for this purpose. Nineteen A-6Bs were converted from A-6A airframes and were tested, like this aircraft, in the US. A few reached combat units and joined the A-6A in operations against North Vietnam. [*Grumman*]

17. Rare view of an A-6B Intruder, minus the missiles for which this variant was designed but serving in an operational unit. Aircraft 151591 of VA-34, 'Blue Blasters', at NAS Oceana, Virginia, in June 1974. Just visible are tiny bumps around the rear circumference of the radome, an identifying feature of the B model. [*Jerry Geer*]

18. The A-6C is another 'odd mod' in the Intruder series. The aircraft was equipped with special electronic TRIM (Rails-Road Interdiction Multi-Sensor) equipment for operations against North Vietnamese supply routes. This package of equipment included FLIR (Forward-Looking Infra-Red), LLLTV (Low Light-Level Television), and the Black Crow device which detected truck exhausts. Similar efforts against the Ho Chi Minh Trail were undertaken by four AP-2H Neptunes, but the A-6C never reached operational service. [*Grumman*]

19

19. Early in the Intruder's career, an A-6A was converted for trials as an in-flight refuelling tanker with a rather crude hose system. Based on the success of these tests, the Navy gave Grumman the go-ahead to develop the KA-6D tanker and the first example, seen here, flew on 16 April 1970. The KA-6D tanker deleted all systems operated by the bombardier-navigator and replaced them with re-fuelling gear, leaving a rather 'plain Jane' right-hand seat in the aircraft. [*Grumman*]

20

20. The KA-6D tanker version usually has some kind of stripe painted around the rear fuselage behind the national insignia, and is often seen flying with four external wing tanks. Aircraft 151589, seen approaching to land at NAS Roosevelt Roads, Puerto Rico, on 20 July 1979, belongs to the 'Sunday Punchers' of

21

VA-75, which was the first Fleet squadron to operate the Intruder. [*USN*]

21. KA-6D Intruder in flight. Almost as soon as they were available, KA-6Ds were deployed to carrier air wings in combat in South-East Asia, where they supplanted and eventually replaced the Douglas KA-3B Skywarrior. This tanker belongs to VA-196 'Main Battery', home-based at NAS Whidbey Island, Washington. [*USN*]

22. Grumman proposed versions of the Intruder airframe for various other roles, including a USAF requirement for a strike aircraft. The only one which reached the full-scale mock-up stage was the very successful four-seat, electronic warfare aircraft developed from the Intruder, the EA-6B Prowler. Actually developed from the EA-6A with the latter's bulged fairing atop the vertical tail, the EA-6B was completed in mock-up form in about late 1967. [*Grumman*]

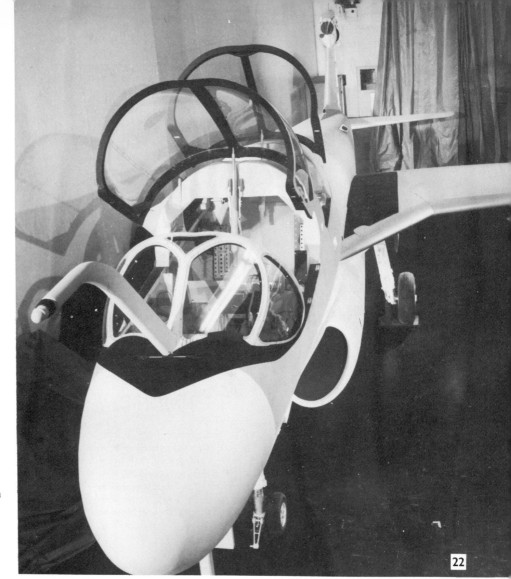

23. Another view of the full-scale EA-6B Prowler mock-up at Grumman's Long Island facility. Note that the Prowler retains many of the features of the A-6 Intruder, including the hook-like air refuelling probe extending forward from and above the windshield. The Prowler was designed to jam enemy radars and communications. The lifelike Prowler mock-up was built without wingtips and tucked in a corner where it was viewed by Navy inspectors. [*Grumman*]

24. The prototype Grumman EA-6B Prowler, aircraft 149481, makes its maiden flight – with 'candy stripe' pitot tube out front and trailing an antenna from the upper rear of the vertical fin – at Calverton, New York, on 25 May 1968 with Don King at the controls. This aircraft, and one more which followed, were converted from A-6A Intruder airframes. Additional Prowlers, including those still in production, are 'new-build' aircraft. The EA-6B carries a pilot and three electronic warfare officers. [Grumman]

25. 'Smart' bomber, Vietnam style. Three

A-6As were adapted to carry the banana-shaped AVQ-10 Pave Knife laser target designator (centreline), and these saw action with VA-145 'Swordsmen' during 1972. [Ford Aerospace via A. Thornborough]

26. While the Intruder was still being evaluated, the USA became deeply involved in war in South-East Asia. Lacking any other warplane capable of operating in bad weather — and embarrassed by the USAF's limited success in doing so with the F-105F Thunderchief — the Navy rushed the A-6A Intruder into service, even though the DIANE electronics system was still not fully ready. Soon the shape of the ungainly Intruder, as illustrated in this close-up of side number 522, became a familiar sight in the Fleet. [*USN*]

27 and 28. Over the South China Sea in July 1968, a formation of A-6A Intruders from the USS *Constellation* (CVA-64) heads towards targets in North Vietnam. These belong to VA-196 'Main Battery'. The black radome associated with early Intruder operations is evident here, as is a generous load of bombs intended for Ho Chi Minh's followers. Beneath the word 'Navy' on the fuselage, the perforated dive brakes have been wired shut, having been replaced by wingtip flaps. [*USN*]

29. Combat. Another July 1968 view of two 'Main Battery' VA-196 Intruders en route from *Constellation* towards North Vietnam. From this angle, fences which channel airflow over the wings are evident. The Intruder could fly to a target 550 miles away, spend ten minutes in the target area, and return to its carrier. Navy pilots and bombardier-navigators were more apprehensive during the carrier landing phase than while confronting Hanoi's defences. [*USN*]

30. On 25 April 1972, with combat operations against North Vietnam being stepped up following President Nixon's decision to mine Haiphong harbour – using Intruders – carrier operations are hectic. This view, aboard the USS *Constellation* (CVA-64), shows A-6A Intruders being readied for what became the final round of fighting in Vietnam. [*USN*]

31. The Marine Corps had a strong interest in the A-6 Intruder right from the start. In addition to taking on the EA-6A electronic warfare version (which was not, until many years later, used by the Navy), the Marines moved quickly to equip their medium attack squadrons with A-6A Intruders. This gaggle belongs to the 'Bengals' of VMA(AW)-224 and is depicted over MCAS Cherry Point, North Carolina, on 28 June 1967. By that date, both Navy and Marine squadrons were employing the Intruder in combat in South-East Asia. [USMC]

32. The beginning of a combat mission. An A-6A belonging to the 'Bats' of VMA(AW)-242, far from its traditional home base at El Toro, California, launches from Da Nang, South Vietnam, with a full load of bombs. Note bat insignia on rudder. Bureau number 152595, like so many others, survived the war and soldiered on afterwards. [USMC]

33. End of a mission. In a view which dramatically shows the Intruder's wing-tip speed brakes, a Marine Corps A-6A of VMA(AW)-533, alias the 'Hawks', makes a hook-arrested landing at Chu Lai, South Vietnam, in December 1967. Chu Lai was a difficult airfield to fight a war from, being paved mostly with pierced steel SATS (Short Airfield, Tactical Support) planking and was never equipped with proper communications and administrative support. The all-weather capability of Marine A-6As was important in both North and South Vietnam. [USMC]

34. A-6A Intruder 152623 of Marine Corps squadron VMA(AW)-121, 'Green Knights', at MCAS Cherry Point, North Carolina, on 13 April 1971. The complex wing fold mechanism of the A-6A Intruder is evident here. In 1989 the Marines decided to give up their Intruder fleet in a move to acquire the F-18D(CR) Hornet two-seat night attack aircraft, and VMA(AW)-121, now redesignated VMFA(AW)-121, became the first to receive the Hornet, in 1989. [*Jim Sullivan*]

35. Another view of a VMA(AW)-121 'Green Knights' A-6A Intruder in flight during the Vietnam war years, this time near Cherry Point on 29 November 1971. Throughout the 1960s and 1970s, Intruders wore the standard Navy/Marine paintscheme of grey on top, white on the undersides. This was to give way to a dirtier 'tactical grey' in the 1980s. VMA(AW)-121 has another unusual event in its history, having served as part of the carrier air wing aboard the USS *Ranger* (CV-61) – unusual for a Marine Corps squadron. [*USMC*]

36. The EA-6A Intruder electronic warfare platform, which was developed solely for the Marine Corps, although Navy units picked up a few in later years. Composite Reconnaissance Squadron Three, or VMCJ-3, was one of three squadrons that operated a mixed force of RF-4B Phantoms and EA-6As until 1975 when the two types were separated into different

units. Note the bulged fairing atop the vertical fin for electronics equipment. The fold-down ladder used by the right-seater to climb aboard is also evident in this view. [*Robert L. Lawson*]

37. A carrier deck, in the colourful post-Vietnam 1970s. A glance at this cluttered view tells us that this carrier air wing has two squadrons of F-14 Tomcats, two of A-7 Corsairs, and the sole medium attack squadron of A-6 Intruders, as well as an EA-6B Prowler detachment. The Intruders are the improved A-6E model, which first flew on 23 January 1970. The Intruders belong to VA-34 'Blue Blasters'. The two EA-6Bs visible in this view belong to the 'Wizards' of VAQ-33. [*Grumman*]

38. With a cloud-covered land mass in the background, A-6A Intruders from the USS *Franklin D. Roosevelt* (CVA-42) tuck into formation during an August 1969 practice mission over the east coast of the United States. The squadron is VA-176 'Thunderbolts', normally shore-based at NAS Oceana, Virginia. This was the era of high-visibility markings on grey-white aircraft, and bureau number 152905 (foreground) and companions have on their tails a stylized streak of lightning together with a cluster of vertical stars. [*USN/William R. Curtsinger*]

39. Grumman's A-6A Intruder, although already blooded in combat, was still very much a new aeroplane when it appeared at an open house at Edwards AFB, California, on 18 May 1969. Bureau number 155644 belongs to VAH-123 'Professionals', an A-3 Skywarrior unit which served as the initial Intruder RAG (replacement air group), or training squadron, until VA-128 'Golden Warriors' could be formed. Both Intruder training squadrons were home-ported at NAS Whidbey Island, Washington, while training duties on the East Coast were performed by VA-42 'Green Pawns' at NAS Oceana, Virginia. [*William E. Johnson*]

40. An EA-6A 'Electric Intruder' belonging to the Strike Test Directorate (STD) at the Naval Air Test Center, Patuxent River, Maryland, photographed on 21 April 1971. Although live missile tests

are not normally carried out at Pax, this aircraft – with everything opened up – has an AIM-78A Standard ARM missile hanging from the left outboard pylon. EA-6As were employed for electronic warfare missions in Vietnam but were not used to attack enemy SAM sites with this missile. [*Roger F. Besecker*]

41. Yet another KA-6D flight-refuelling version of the Intruder, this time with the band around the rear fuselage usually found on the tanker version. Bureau number 151813 of the 'Boomers' of VA-165, assigned to the USS *Constellation* (CVA-64), was seen on a visit to NAS North Island, California, on 18 June 1974. All West Coast/Pacific Fleet Intruders made their home port at NAS Whidbey Island, Washington, in the cloudy and rainy Pacific north-west, when not at sea. Weather at Whidbey was generally so bad

that the 'all-weather' Intruder could fly only 97 per cent of the time. [*Duane A. Kasulka*]

42. Perhaps the definitive portrait of an Intruder in the early 1970s. This KA-6D tanker of VA-65 'Tigers' from the USS *Independence* (CVA-62) wears the classic grey-white Navy paint scheme and prominent markings of the period. Note that the squadron name even appears on the wingtanks.

All East Coast/Atlantic Fleet Intruders were home-ported at NAS Oceana, Virginia, when not embarked in a carrier. The right-hand crew member had no real duties in the KA-6D tanker, which offered minimal controls on the starboard side. [*USN*]

43. Few squadrons had an emblem more ominous than the 'Bats' of VMA (AW)-242, one of the early Marine Corps A-6A

Intruder squadrons, seen here during a visit to NAS Miramar, California, on 15 March 1975. Underside white and white radome seem to blend into the grey of the upper portion of the aircraft in this view. Yet another thunderbolt, running through the 'DT' tailcode, is barely visible. Like the Navy, the Marine Corps operated the A-6A successfully before moving on to the definitive A-6E Intruder. [*Robert L. Lawson*]

43

44. On the eastern side of the country, Intruder lead-in training was provided by squadron VMAT(AW)-202, which operated from 1979 to 1986 without ever acquiring an official nickname. A-6A Intruder bureau number 152641 is seen at its home base, MCAS Cherry Point, North Carolina, on 20 July 1972. [*Jim Sullivan*]

45. Another view of an A-6A Intruder of Marine Corps training squadron VMFAT(AW)-202, this time at MCAS Beaufort, South Carolina, on 12 June 1972. Visible in this view of bureau number 152620 are the perforations (below the word 'Marines') in the fuselage dive brakes, which have now been wired shut and replaced by wingtip speed brakes. [*Frank R. MacSorley*]

46. The 'Green Knights' of VMA(AW)-121 were one of the first Marine Corps squadrons to operate the Intruder in about 1970, and one of the last to convert from the Intruder in 1990. Bureau number 155581 wears the distinctive knight's head on its rudder and is seen at MCAS Cherry Point, North Carolina, on 12 June 1972. Note the clean lines of the clamshell canopy, which slides straight back on rails. [*Frank R. MacSorley*]

47. Wings folded, ladder down, T-shirted ground crew at work, A-6A Intruder 154168 poses for veteran photographer Jim Sullivan at MCAS Cherry Point, North Carolina, on 20 July 1972. The 'Polka Dots' of VMA(AW)-332 are one of the least-

47

publicized of Marine Corps Intruder squadrons, although they operated the aircraft for several years. Note that the aircraft is obtaining cooling for its internal systems from a

ground unit attached via a long hose. [*Jim Sullivan*]

48. In the early 1970s the US Navy and Marine Corps tested a variety of carrier-style launch and recovery

systems for tactical aircraft, including this catapult on runway 1–8 at the liaison Marine facility at Bogue, North Carolina. Purpose was to provide realistic carrier training

without a carrier. Bureau number 154162, an A-6A Intruder of VMA(AW)-121 'Green Knights', is seen being run up on the launch catapult on 18 January 1973. [*USMC*]

48

Specification

Grumman A-6A Intruder

Type: Two-seat carrier-based medium attack aircraft
Powerplant: Two 9,300lb (4,218kg) thrust non-afterburning Pratt & Whitney J52-P-8A turbojets
Performance: Maximum speed (clean) 685mph (1,102km/h) at sea-level, or 625mph (1,006km/h) at height; service ceiling 41,660ft (12,700m); ferry range with external fuel approx. 3,100 miles (4,890km)
Weights: Empty 25,684lb (11, 650kg); maximum take-off 60,400lb (27,397kg)
Dimensions: Span 53ft (16.15m); length 54ft 7in (16.64m); height 15ft 7in (4.75m); wing area 528.9sqft (49.1m^2)
Armament: Five stores stations, each rated at 3,600lb (1,633kg), with maximum total load of 18,000lb (8,164kg)

A-6 Intruder and EA-6B Prowler Squadrons

* Indicates squadrons which were no longer in service or had converted to other aircraft by the beginning of the 1990s. At the beginning of 1990, the US Marine Corps announced plans to replace its A-6 fleet with F/A-18D(CR) Hornets.

** Indicates fleet replenishment squadrons (FRS), formerly known as replacement air groups (RAG), which train pilots, bombardier-navigators and electronic warfare officers prior to their assignment to Fleet units.

1. US Navy A-6 Intruder Squadrons

Unit	Nickname	Home Port
VA-34	Blue Blasters	NAS Oceana, Virginia
VA-35	Black Panthers	Oceana
VA-36	Roadrunners	Oceana
VA-42**	Green Pawns	Oceana
VA-52	Knight Riders	NAS Whidbey Island, Washington
VA-55	Warhorses	Oceana
VA-65	Tigers	Oceana
VA-75	Sunday Punchers	Oceana
VA-85	Black Falcons	Oceana
VA-95	Green Lizards	Whidbey
VA-115	Arabs	NAF Atsugi, Japan
VA-123*	Professionals	Whidbey
VA-128**	Golden Intruders	Whidbey
VA-145	Swordsmen	Whidbey
VA-155	Silver Foxes	Atsugi
VA-165	Boomers	Whidbey
VA-176	Thunderbolts	Oceana
VA-185	Knighthawks	Whidbey
VA-196	Main Battery	Whidbey
VX-5	Vampires	NAS China Lake, California

2. US Navy and Marine Corps EA-6A Intruder Squadrons

VMCJ-1*	Eyes of the Corps	MCAS Iwakuni, Japan
VMCJ-2*	Playboys	MCAS Cherry Point, North Carolina
VMCJ-3*		MCAS El Toro, California
VMAQ-2	Playboys	Cherry Point
VMAQ-4	Seahawks	Whidbey
VAQ-33	Firebirds	NAS Norfolk, Virginia
VAQ-209	Star Warriors	Norfolk
VAQ-309	Axemen	Whidbey

3. US Marine Corps A-6 Intruder Squadrons

VMA(AW)-121*	Green Lizards	Cherry Point
VMAT(AW)-202*	**	Cherry Point
VMA(AW)-224	Bengals	Cherry Point
VMA(AW)-225	Vagabonds	El Toro
VMA(AW)-242	Bats	El Toro
VMA(AW)-332	Polka Dots	Cherry Point
VMA(AW)-533	Hawks	Iwakuni

4. US Navy and Marine Corps EA-6B Prowler Squadrons

VAQ-129**	Vikings	Whidbey
VAQ-130	Zappers	Whidbey
VAQ-131	Lancers	Whidbey
VAQ-132	Scorpions	Whidbey
VAQ-133	Wizards	Whidbey
VAQ-134	Garudas	Whidbey
VAQ-135	Black Ravens	Whidbey
VAQ-136	Gauntlets	Whidbey
VAQ-137	Rooks	Whidbey
VAQ-138	Yellow Jackets	Whidbey
VAQ-139	Cougars	Whidbey
VAQ-140		Whidbey
VAQ-141		Whidbey
VAQ-142		Whidbey
VMAQ-2	Playboys	MCAS Cherry Point, North Carolina
VAQ-309	Axemen	Whidbey (Reserve)

A. The Grumman EA-6B Prowler has become the standard electronic warfare aircraft on US Navy carrier decks and has participated in combat operations from Vietnam to Libya. Although all Prowlers look the same externally, frequent updating of the 'black boxes' and electronic wizardry inside the aircraft has resulted in no newer than five major variants. [*US Navy*]

B. The ADVCAP (Advanced Capability) EA-6B Prowler is the latest version of this electronic warfare aircraft and is seen on its first flight, 29 October 1989, with Grumman test pilot John Leslie at the controls. Bureau number 156482 is actually a test aircraft, and the first operational ADVCAP Prowler is scheduled to join the Fleet in 1992. [*Grumman*]

C. An A-6E Intruder of VA-145 'Swordsmen' comes aboard a Pacific Fleet carrier in 1976 in a sombre view which reflects the gloomy weather in which the Intruder was meant to operate. The A-7 Corsair in the foreground has been replaced as the Navy's standard light attack aircraft, but the Intruder continues in the medium attack role. [*Robert F. Dorr*]

D. VMFAT(AW)-202 was the US Marine Corps' training squadron, or RAG (replacement air group) for Intruder pilots. The colourful markings seen on aircraft 157003 were worn for only a brief period and the squadron has now passed into history, without ever having had an official nickname. [*US Navy*]

E. Seen aboard the USS *America* (CVA-66) on 12 September 1982, A-6E Intruder 155691, 'AB-517', belongs to the 'Blue

Blasters' of VA-34. The thoroughly choreographed efforts of deck crew members are an essential part of the Intruder story. [*Steve Daniels*]

F. A flight-deck view of the A-6E model, which differed from earlier Intruder attack bombers only in its internal systems. Although the 1970s paint scheme of grey over white is still being illustrated, this view was taken on 16 April 1986 aboard the carrier USS *Coral Sea* (CV-43) when hostilities with Libya were near a peak. The squadron is VA-55, 'Warhorses'. [*USN*]

G. During combat operations against Libya in April 1986, an A-6E TRAM Intruder is moved forward

on the flight deck of the USS *Coral Sea* (CV-43).

Intruders struck targets around Benghazi while

USAF F-111s attacked Tripoli. [*US Navy*]

H. A pair of drab grey Intruders in 1983. [*US Navy*]

I. Adorned in the 'plain Jane' markings and laden with Mark 83 500lb bombs, this A-6E Intruder is on a low-level training mission in 1983. [*US Navy*]

J. On a rare carrier deployment, an A-6E Intruder is seen aboard the USS *Midway* (CVA-41) in December 1976. 159309 belongs to squadron VMA (AW)-332, the 'Polka Dots', usually stationed at MCAS Cherry Point, North Carolina. [*Steve Daniels*]

K. An A-6E Intruder belonging to training squadron VA-42, the 'Green Pawns', at NAS Oceana, Virginia, on 20 October 1977. The radome of this aircraft appears to be showing its age. [*Robert F. Dorr*]

L. Close-up of the business end of A-6E Intruder 157014, seen at the Naval Air Test Center, NAS Patuxent River, Maryland on 27 February 1987. [*Robert F. Dorr*]

M. VMA(AW)-533, the 'Hawks' was the first Marine Corps squadron to employ the Intruder operationally, and has spent much of its career at MCAS Iwakuni, Japan. This sunset shot was apparently taken aboard the USS *Midway* (CVA-41) in the 1970s. [*US Navy*]

N. Another carrier-borne view of the Intruder. Aboard the USS *Constellation* (CV-64), A-6E Intruder 155664 is moved into position. The squadron is VA-165, nicknamed 'Boomers' and home-ported at NAS Whidbey Island, Washington. [*Chris Pocock*]

O. The Intruder is seldom seen in formation on actual combat missions as its all-weather capability makes it ideal for 'lone wolf' missions. These Intruders belong to the East Coast training squadron, VA-34 'Green Pawns'. [*US Navy*]

P. Launching from the USS *Independence* (CVA-62), A-6E Intruder 155715 of VA-176 'Thunderbolts' wears the high-visibility markings which characterized Navy aircraft until the early 1980s. [*US Navy*]

Q. A-6A Intruder 154162, assigned to the Pacific Missile Test Range (PMTC) at Point Mugu, California, acting as a 'chase' aircraft in the Tomahawk cruise missile programme. [*US Navy*]

R. EA-6B Prowler electronic warfare aircraft 156478 has been part of the test stable at NATC Patuxent River, Maryland, for many years. This view of the very bright 156478 was taken by the author on 31 March 1977. [*Robert F. Dorr*]

S. Had it been built in larger numbers, the A-6B Intruder with AGM-78 Standard ARM missiles might have replaced the Douglas A-4E Skyhawk with AGM-45 Shrikes as the principal carrier-borne weapon against North Vietnam's SAM sites. Instead, the A-6B became little more than a curiosity, with one or two airframes distributed among the Navy's A-6 squadrons. Some were later converted to A-6E standard, although the E model is covered in this book (see plates 16—17). [*Grumman*]

T. A recent view of an air-to-air hook-up with the KA-6D performing its function as a tanker. The drogue, or refuelling receptacle, is lowered by hose which extends from a fairing in the ventral area of the KA-6D, and the refuelling aircraft 'plugs in' using a probe — which in the case of the Intruder is a non-retractable device on the forward fuselage. These aircraft belong to VA-165 'Boomers' and are flying over the American South-West. [*Grumman*]

Aircraft Dimensions

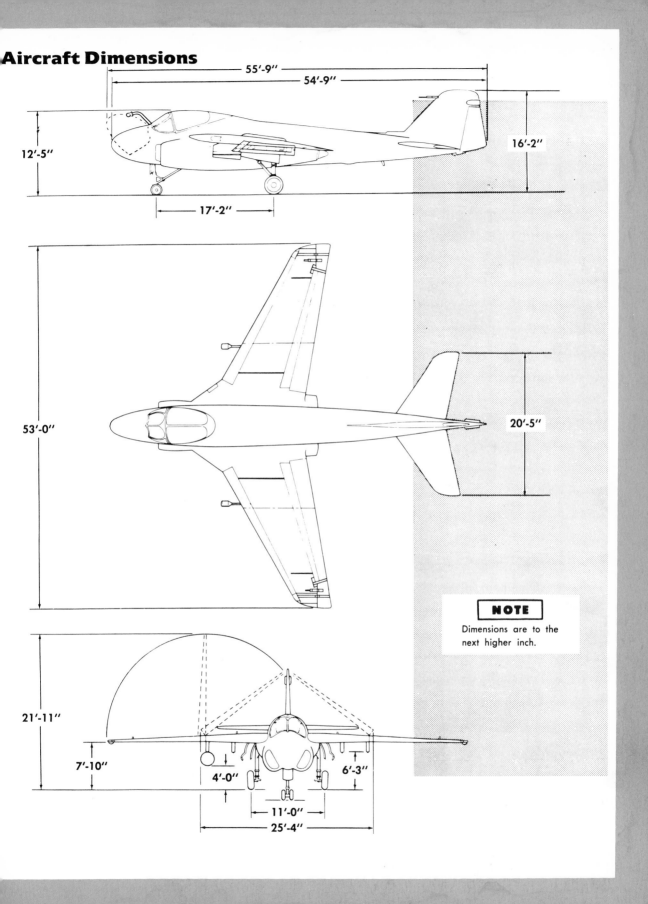

55'-9"
54'-9"
12'-5"
16'-2"
17'-2"
53'-0"
20'-5"

NOTE

Dimensions are to the next higher inch.

21'-11"
7'-10"
4'-0"
6'-3"
11'-0"
25'-4"

Paint Scheme

Acrylic Camouflage Light Gull Gray
Item (32).

Acrylic Gloss Insignia
White Item (32).

Epoxy-Polyamide Coating
Item (20)

Light Gull Gray Walkway
Compound Item (15).

Do Not Paint Area.

White Rain Erosion Coating
item (7).

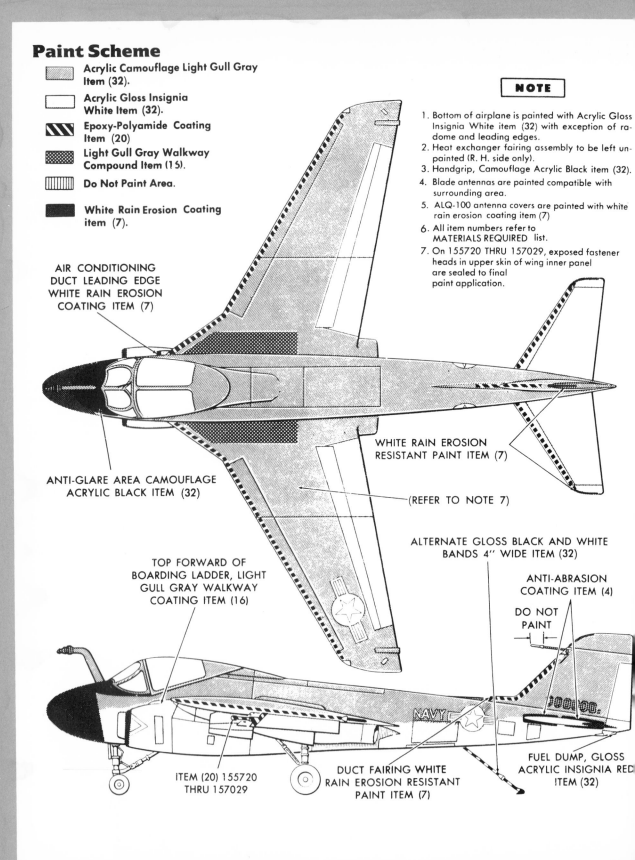

AIR CONDITIONING
DUCT LEADING EDGE
WHITE RAIN EROSION
COATING ITEM (7)

ANTI-GLARE AREA CAMOUFLAGE
ACRYLIC BLACK ITEM (32)

WHITE RAIN EROSION
RESISTANT PAINT ITEM (7)

(REFER TO NOTE 7)

TOP FORWARD OF
BOARDING LADDER, LIGHT
GULL GRAY WALKWAY
COATING ITEM (16)

ALTERNATE GLOSS BLACK AND WHITE
BANDS 4" WIDE ITEM (32)

ANTI-ABRASION
COATING ITEM (4)

DO NOT
PAINT

ITEM (20) 155720
THRU 157029

DUCT FAIRING WHITE
RAIN EROSION RESISTANT
PAINT ITEM (7)

FUEL DUMP, GLOSS
ACRYLIC INSIGNIA RED
ITEM (32)

NAVY

Low-Visibility Paint Scheme

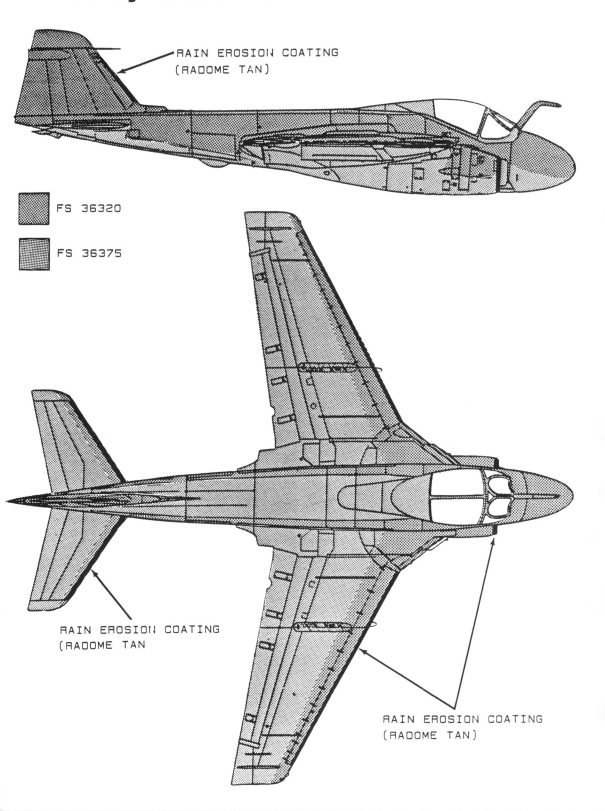

RAIN EROSION COATING
(RADOME TAN)

FS 36320

FS 36375

RAIN EROSION COATING
(RADOME TAN

RAIN EROSION COATING
(RADOME TAN)

General Arrangement

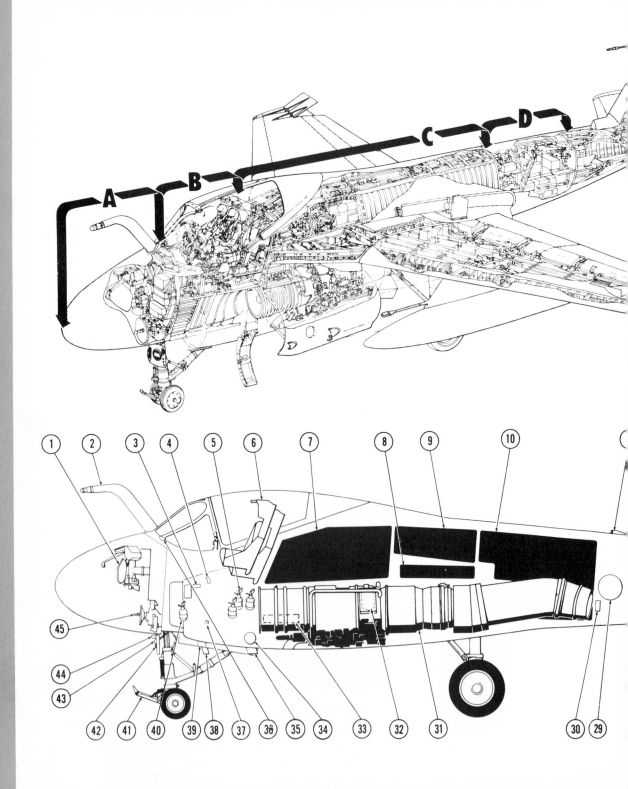

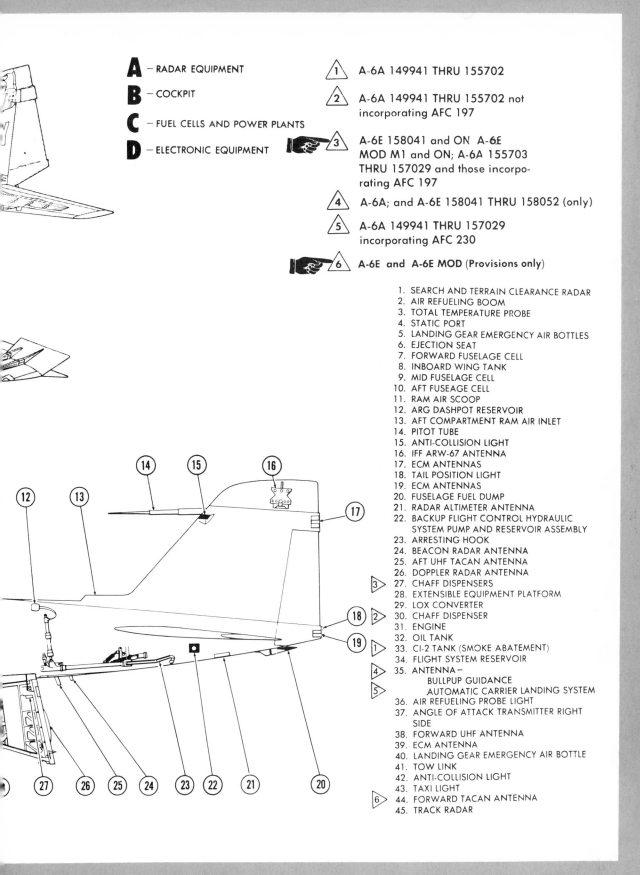

A – RADAR EQUIPMENT

B – COCKPIT

C – FUEL CELLS AND POWER PLANTS

D – ELECTRONIC EQUIPMENT

△1 A-6A 149941 THRU 155702

△2 A-6A 149941 THRU 155702 not incorporating AFC 197

☞ △3 A-6E 158041 and ON A-6E MOD M1 and ON; A-6A 155703 THRU 157029 and those incorporating AFC 197

△4 A-6A; and A-6E 158041 THRU 158052 (only)

△5 A-6A 149941 THRU 157029 incorporating AFC 230

☞ △6 A-6E and A-6E MOD (Provisions only)

1. SEARCH AND TERRAIN CLEARANCE RADAR
2. AIR REFUELING BOOM
3. TOTAL TEMPERATURE PROBE
4. STATIC PORT
5. LANDING GEAR EMERGENCY AIR BOTTLES
6. EJECTION SEAT
7. FORWARD FUSELAGE CELL
8. INBOARD WING TANK
9. MID FUSELAGE CELL
10. AFT FUSEAGE CELL
11. RAM AIR SCOOP
12. ARG DASHPOT RESERVOIR
13. AFT COMPARTMENT RAM AIR INLET
14. PITOT TUBE
15. ANTI-COLLISION LIGHT
16. IFF ARW-67 ANTENNA
17. ECM ANTENNAS
18. TAIL POSITION LIGHT
19. ECM ANTENNAS
20. FUSELAGE FUEL DUMP
21. RADAR ALTIMETER ANTENNA
22. BACKUP FLIGHT CONTROL HYDRAULIC SYSTEM PUMP AND RESERVOIR ASSEMBLY
23. ARRESTING HOOK
24. BEACON RADAR ANTENNA
25. AFT UHF TACAN ANTENNA
26. DOPPLER RADAR ANTENNA
▷3 27. CHAFF DISPENSERS
28. EXTENSIBLE EQUIPMENT PLATFORM
29. LOX CONVERTER
▷2 30. CHAFF DISPENSER
31. ENGINE
32. OIL TANK
▷1 33. CI-2 TANK (SMOKE ABATEMENT)
34. FLIGHT SYSTEM RESERVOIR
▷4 35. ANTENNA –
        BULLPUP GUIDANCE
▷5   AUTOMATIC CARRIER LANDING SYSTEM
36. AIR REFUELING PROBE LIGHT
37. ANGLE OF ATTACK TRANSMITTER RIGHT SIDE
38. FORWARD UHF ANTENNA
39. ECM ANTENNA
40. LANDING GEAR EMERGENCY AIR BOTTLE
41. TOW LINK
42. ANTI-COLLISION LIGHT
43. TAXI LIGHT
▷6 44. FORWARD TACAN ANTENNA
45. TRACK RADAR

49. The 'Polka Dots' of VMA(AW)-332 enjoyed a brief but happy period when they were permitted to adorn wingtanks and rudder panels with their namesake. Seen with wings folded on the cluttered flight line at MCAS Cherry Point, North Carolina, on 13 April 1971, is bureau number 154167. Note tie-down rope behind nose wheel. [*Jim Sullivan*]

50. Leaving heat thermals in its path as it lands at MCAS Cherry Point, North Carolina, on 12 April 1971, A-6A Intruder 155650 belongs to VMA(AW)-224, the 'Bengals'. The Intruder's pilot sits high relative to the position of the aircraft and enjoys excellent visibility during all phases of flight. Note wingtip speed brakes in extended position. [*Jim Sullivan*]

51. The sword prominently displayed on the tail of bureau number 155669 denotes the 'Swordsmen' of VA-145, who shared their nickname with an F-4 Phantom squadron, VF-32. This 1 October 1975 view was taken during a cruise aboard the USS *Ranger* (CVA-61) and shows the A-6A Intruder with wing and fuselage centre-line fuel tanks. [*USN*]

52. The Pacific north-west near Whidbey Island can be a striking backdrop for an Intruder on a nice day. We have seen bureau number 155669 winging along carrying a load of fuel tanks (photo 51). With snow on the mountain slopes in the background, the Navy's grey-white paint scheme on the same aircraft seems to blend with the passing scenery. [*USN*]

53. We shift now from the A-6A to the A-6E model, which was externally indistinguishable. Tropical thunderheads have built up in the distance at MCAS Kaneohe Bay, Hawaii, in June 1981 as ground crewmen work on Marine Corps A-6E 154129. The era of colourful markings on Navy and Marine aircraft is drawing to an end and the 'Polka Dots' of VMA(AW)-332 look far plainer than when seen previously. Kaneohe Bay was a fighter base brimming with F-4 Phantoms. The Intruders were pausing between their home base at MCAS Cherry Point, North Carolina, and a 'forward deployment' to MCAS Iwakuni, Japan, where, on a rotational basis, one attack squadron remained ready for possible trouble in Korea. [*USN*]

54. The 'Green Pawns' of VA-42 are the East Coast/Atlantic Fleet replacement training unit, once known in Navy parlance as an RAG (Replacement Air Group) and more recently as an FRS (Fleet Replenishment Squadron), and they were rightly miffed when their nickname appeared in one Intruder publication as the 'Green Prawns'. Still adorned in classic Navy grey-white, A-6E Intruder 155658 cruises in clean condition over a sky of light, scattered clouds. [*Grumman*]

55. East Coast Intruders on the move. The 'Blue Blasters' of VA-34, when not operating aboard a carrier — here, they are assigned to the USS *John F. Kennedy* — are home-based at NAS Oceana, Virginia, with the re-mainder of the East Coast/Atlantic Fleet Intruder community. Barely per-ceptible on this pair of 'Blue Blasters' is a small fairing for a cooling intake located just ahead and to the left of the base of the vertical fin. This is one of the few features which distinguish an A-6E, shown here, from the earlier A-6A. [*USN*]

56. On the busy ramp at NAS Oceana, Virginia, not far from the boardwalk and sandy shores of Vir-ginia Beach, KA-6D In-truder 152919 is seen tied down and held in reserve in April 1974. The Intruder was assigned to the carrier air wing aboard the USS *Roosevelt* (CVA-42), which was retired from active service that year. Note mailed fist and lightning bolt from the glory days of naval aircraft markings. [*Robert F. Dorr*]

57. An A-6A Intruder (not a KA-6D tanker) carrying a centre-line Douglas D-704 in-flight refuelling pod as well as wingtanks, enabling the attack version of the Intruder to function on a temporary basis as a tanker. Bureau number 155683 of the 'Boomers' of VA-165 is seen during a visit to NAS North Island, California, on 18 June 1974. The complex wing-fold mechanism of the Intruder never ceases to amaze onlookers. [*Duane A. Kasulka*]

57

58. 'Boomers' in the air. By the time this picture was taken on 7 March 1980, the squadron was flying the A-6E model, with the aircraft in the background carrying the same D-704 refuelling pod seen in the previous photo (photo No 57). VA-165's tail marking also has changed somewhat since the 1974 view. The squadron was aboard the USS *Constellation* (CVA-64) at this time. [*USN*]

59

59. The A-6E Intruder in its natural setting, on the lift of a carrier at sea, in this case the nuclear-powered USS *Enterprise* (CVAN-65) in the early 1980s. The squadron is VA-196 'Main Battery'.

The Intruder was by no means the easiest aircraft to maintain or to move around a crowded carrier deck, but two aircraft could fit quite comfortably on a lift. [*USN*]

60. The US Marine Corps converted from the A-6A to the A-6E Intruder in the 1970s, but the 'Green Knights' of VMA(AW)-121 were still flying the A-6A model when this photo was taken from a Navy

trainer at NAS Whiting Field, Florida, in 1980. Bureau number 155638 wears the standard grey/white paint scheme of the period and is on a routine flight. [*USMC*]

60

beneath the nose. The first flight of bureau number 155673, development aircraft for the TRAM version, took place on 29 October 1974. The turret contains both infra-red and laser equipment and is partly retractable. TRAM provides the crew with real-time television imagery of non-visual or radar targets. [*Grumman*]

61

62

63. The A-6E TRAM Intruder development aircraft, bureau number 155673, banks over the sea near Grumman's Long Island home. The TRAM system integrates FLIR (forward-looking infra-red) and laser sensors with target identification, tracking and ranging in any light or weather conditions. The bombardier-navigator is thus able to locate the target at greater distances than before and to plan a radar approach to the target which will permit him to attack with laser-guided bombs, even in the worst possible weather. [*USN*]

61. A stark view of the method of catapult launching pioneered by the A-6 Intruder – attaching the nose wheel to the steam catapult. On 5 May 1983 this A-6E Intruder was being readied for launch from the USS *America* (CV-66). Previously, warplanes were launched via attachments to their main gear or fuselage. [*USN*]

62. The final configuration for the US Navy's medium attack aircraft came with the A-6E TRAM Intruder (Target Recognition Attack, Multi-Sensor), distinguished from other versions by the TRAM turret

63

64

65

66

64. A-6E TRAM Intruder 155648 of VA-145 'Swordsmen' during a sortie from the USS *Kitty Hawk* (CV-63) in 1984, just as the Navy's traditional grey-white paint scheme, shown, was about to be replaced with tactical grey. This aircraft carries a very unusual combination, namely a centre-line D-704 'buddy' refuelling tank plus a Mark 83 2,000lb (907kg) bomb in the aft position on the inboard bomb pylon. In December 1983 Intruders flew a one-off air strike on the Lebanon and one aircraft was shot down by Syrian surface-to-air missiles. [*USN*]

65. The EA-6B Prowler is in many respects only a distant cousin of the A-6 Intruder, but the family lines are obvious. Shown here is the prototype EA-6B, bureau number 149481, which was retained by Grumman for a period for development work. The EA-6B Prowler first saw action against North Vietnam in July 1972 with the 'Lancers' of VAQ-131 aboard the USS

67

Enterprise (CVAN-65), after training was carried out by the 'Vikings' of VAQ-129 at NAS Whidbey Island, Washington. [*Grumman*]

66. The EA-6B Prowler is one of the larger aircraft types to operate from a carrier deck and is by no means easy to bring aboard or to launch when the ship is heaving in rough seas. This view shows a basic EA-6B Prowler, bureau number 158032, after catching the wire for a successful landing aboard the USS *Dwight D. Eisenhower* (CVN-69) on 12 Septem-

ber 1980. Belonging to squadron VAQ-132, the 'Scorpions', this EA-6B is part of a task force that was built up in the Middle East while American hostages were being held in Tehran. [*USN*]

67. Dramatic view of an EA-6B Prowler being launched by the steam catapult of the USS *Independence* (CV-62) off the Lebanese coast on 7 December 1983, just days after an air strike over the Lebanon was flown by A-6s and A-7s to support peacekeeping efforts in Beirut. Bureau number 158649 is the basic EA-6B design

and belongs to the 'Lancers' of VAQ-131. [*USN*]

68. Bureau number 159584 belongs to the second generation of EA-6B Prowlers, known as EXCAP (expanded capability) aircraft with improved systems, first deployed to the Mediterranean in January 1974. EXCAP Prowlers differ from the first-generation or 'basic' aircraft in being able to carry out the electronic warfare role against enemy radars in eight frequency bands instead of four. This machine was on display at an air show in England. [*Robert F. Dorr*]

68

69

69. EA-6B Prowler EXCAP aircraft, bureau number 159586, of the 'Yellow Jackets' of VAQ-138, seen on 11 May 1978 during a visit to NAS Oceana, Virginia, while on a cruise aboard the USS *Dwight D. Eisenhower* (CVN-69). Since only a detachment of Prowlers, often two aircraft, serves in a carrier air wing, the same squadron could have aircraft aboard more then one ship at a time. A stylized 'E' for excellence award appears on the fuel tank of this aircraft attired in the standard Navy grey/white paint scheme. [*USN/J. E. Michaels*]

70. Just discernible in this flight deck view is the 'sawtooth' found at the base of the Prowler's L-shaped refuelling probe, an identifying feature of EA-6B Prowlers in the third-generation ICAP 1 (Improved Capability) series and onward. The notch was created by locating an AN/ALQ-125 radar receiver in the base of the probe. Bureau number 158030 belongs to the 'Garudas' of VAQ-134 and is wearing standard grey/white paint aboard the *USS Nimitz* (CVN-68) in April 1980. Note the huge underwing pod which is packed with electronic jamming gear, as well as twin clamshell canopies for the four-man crew. [*USN*]

70

71 and 72. Basic EA-6B Prowler 158031 of VAQ-129 'Vikings', the training squadron located at NAS Whidbey Island, Washington. [*USN*]

71

73. EA-6B Prowler 160788 during US anti-terrorist operations against Libya in 1986. Although the aircraft has 'Saratoga' painted on its fuselage, the first Marine Corps Prowler squadron, VMAQ-2 'Playboys', was actually aboard the USS *America* (CV-66) during March 1986 'Prairie Fire' and April 1986 'El Dorado Canyon' operations against Col. Muamar Khadaffi's Libya. This is also our first look at the one-shade tactical grey paint scheme which replaced the Navy/Marine grey/white scheme in the mid-1980s. [*USN*]

72

73

74. A pair of VAQ-138 'Yellow Jackets' Prowlers on a mission from the USS *Nimitz* (CVN-68) on 10 November 1986. Although side numbers (the three-digit 'plane in group' numbers on the nose, which can change) are painted in black, the remainder of these aircraft's markings are of such low visibility that they can barely be seen, even when only a few feet away. Since the Prowler first appeared, versions known as EXCAP, ICAP 1, ICAP 2, and ADVCAP (Advanced Capability) have appeared, each with significant internal changes but with very little to look for in the way of external identifying features. [*USN*]

75. The same EA-6B Prowler as seen in photo No 73 aboard the USS *America* (CV-66) off the coast of Libya in April 1986; an A-6E Intruder to the right. During operations against Libya, Prowlers jammed communications while Intruders attacked targets near Benghazi and USAF F-111Fs struck Tripoli. [*USN*]

76. Grey against grey. An EA-6B Prowler in the current tactical grey paint scheme flies over a gloomy Pacific north-west. Like the Intruder, the EA-6B Prowler has all-weather capability and can operate when most aircraft types are grounded. [*Grumman*]

77. Aboard the USS *America* (CV-66) during operations against Libya in early 1986, a KA-6D Intruder is seen with an F-14 Tomcat immediately behind. US Navy deck crewmen aboard aircraft-carriers were always unsung heroes, but their job became especially difficult during intense, cyclic operations when aircraft had to be moved quickly under combat conditions. [*USN*]

78. Returning to the two-seat Intruder attack aircraft, this 12 February 1986 view shows an A-6E Intruder, pulled by an MD-3A tractor, aboard the USS *Saratoga* (CV-60) off the coast of Libya, with F-14 Tomcats and A-7 Corsairs in the background. This was the tense period when the US Navy was challenging Col. Khadaffi's 'Line of Death' across the Gulf of Sirte. *Saratoga* was soon joined by *America* and *Coral Sea* for action against Libya. [*USN*]

79. A cluttered view of the third carrier involved in combat operations against Libya in 1986, the USS *Coral Sea* (CV-43), with A-6E Intruders nudged up against the twin tails of F/A-18 Hornets. [*USN*]

80. The men who do the job. Probably the most important of the trio is the plane captain (centre), who regards the A-6E Intruder as his own special trust from the American taxpayer and labours mightily to keep it in the air. Pilot and bombardier-navigator are attired typically in coveralls, G-suits, and harnesses. Note bombs hanging from wing stations on the Intruder behind the three men. [*USN*]

81. An A-6E TRAM Intruder belonging to operation test and evaluation squadron VX-5, 'Vampires', at NAS China Lake, California, in 1983, in the grey/white paint scheme, which has since been discarded. This machine is carrying four McDonnell Douglas AGM-84A Harpoon anti-shipping missiles, which were used operationally for the first time against Libya in 1986. [*USN*]

82. Wingtip flaps open as it approaches the wire of *Coral Sea* for a tailhook landing on 22 March 1986, this A-6E TRAM Intruder carries a warload typical for operations against Libya. Under the starboard wing is a cylindrical device holding CBU-53 Rockeye cluster bombs. Under the port wing are an AGM-84 Harpoon anti-shipping missile (inboard) and AIM-9 Sidewinder air-to-air missile (outboard). The TRAM Intruder is painted in tactical grey. [*USN*]

83. An A-6E Intruder of VA-196 'Main Battery' being launched from the USS *Enterprise* (CVAN-65) during a Pacific Fleet exercise on 13 April 1978. [*USN*]

84

84. Modern-day Intruders on the prowl. In the colourless tactical grey paint scheme which has become standard, two A-6E TRAM Intruders of VA-128 'Golden Intruders' carry Mark 82 500lb (227kg) bombs on a trip to the target range at NAF El Centro, California. The US Navy has sought to have more realistic air-to-ground training to prepare Intruder crews for 'the real thing' and now operates 'Strike University' at Fallon, Nevada, to add to training traditionally carried out at El Centro. [*USN/Robert L. Lawson*]

85

85. During an exercise called 'Cope Thunder' at NAS Cubi Point, Philippines, in January 1988, an A-6E TRAM Intruder taxies out with a load of Mark 82 500lb (227kg) bombs. Ironically, the ability of the Intruder to operate from carrier decks and strike targets hundreds of miles away is one strong alternative to maintaining air and naval bases in the Philippines, which the US is finding politically expensive. [*USN*]

86

86. Tactical grey in formation. On 10 February 1986, at the very time other Intruder squadrons were making ready for action against Libya, these Marine Corps A-6E TRAM Intruders of VMA(AW)-121 'Green Knights' were winging over the American south-west. These aircraft are operating from NAS Fallon, Nevada, where Navy Secretary John Lehman established 'Strike University' to provide realistic air-to-ground exercises. [*USN/ Robert L. Lawson*]

87. Rare indeed is the A-6E TRAM Intruder which visits the United Kingdom. Bureau number 155703, with black side number but otherwise in lacklustre tactical grey, settles on to the runway for an appearance at a British air show in 1985. Carrier landings do not allow the usual 'flare-out' associated with bringing fast jets back to terra firma, and the Intruder makes a rock-hard impact when it hits the runway. [John Dunnell]

88. Intruder and friend. Despite its capabilities, the A-6 Intruder is not usually regarded as much of an air-to-air combatant. But during a cruise by the USS *Ranger* (CV-61) near Japan and Korea, A-6E TRAM Intruder 151820, piloted by Capt Paul Higgins, escorted a Soviet 'Bear'. [USMC]

89. An A-6E TRAM Intruder (foreground) in tactical grey leads two non-TRAM ships on a 17 November 1982 mission carrying laser-guided bombs and cluster bombs. The aircraft belong to the 'Tigers' of VA-65. [USN/ Robert L. Lawson]

87

88

89

90. Bomb-laden A-6E Intruders in tactical grey carrying bombs over the American south-west. [*Grumman*]

90

91. An A-6E TRAM Intruder in tactical grey lands on the deck of the USS *Coral Sea* (CV-43) on 29 January 1986, just before operations against Libya. The TRAM turret located forward of the Intruder's nose landing gear is designed to withstand the shock of a carrier landing. This Intruder has leading-edge flaps and wingtip speed brakes extended. [*USN*]

91

92. Barely discernible behind its canopy, this A-6E TRAM Intruder, bureau number 161685, displays two 'kill' markings for Libyan missile boats destroyed by Intruder-fired AGM-84A Harpoon missiles in April 1986. The aircraft is seen at NAS Oceana, Virginia, on 19 April 1986. [*Joseph G. Handelman, DDS*]

92

93. Two A-6E TRAM Intruders on a mission from the USS *Dwight D. Eisenhower* (CVN-69) in August 1983. [*USN*]

93

94. When this picture was taken, it depicted the aircraft of the future. The fuselage section of A-6F Intruder full-scale development (FSD) aircraft No 1, bureau number 162183, is being moved to the front of Grumman's Calverton, New York, assembly line for final assembly. No one could have guessed that the A-6F programme, and the subsequent A-6G, would be cancelled in the late 1980s at the very time when the Intruder had reached full maturity. The A-6F was to introduce new engines and totally new internal systems, including new cockpit instruments, to the Intruder design. [*Grumman*]

95. Grumman A-6F Intruder II making its first flight in 1987, replacing the familiar J52 turbojets with non-afterburning 10,700lb (4,853kg) thrust General Electric F404-GE-400D smokeless engines. The F model was to have inverse synthetic aperture radar (ISAR) and other dramatic improvements over the Fleet's A-6E TRAM Intruder. The US Navy has since committed itself heavily to the forthcoming General Dynamics A-12 Avenger II as its next medium attack aircraft, but many believe that the decision to cancel the A-6F and never-built A-6G was premature. [*Grumman*]

96. The future that never was. Two A-6F Intruder II full-scale development aircraft in flight after the programme was cancelled in 1989. Note the different shape of the cooling scoops just forward of the vertical fin. The lead aircraft has a pitot probe not found on the second. [*Grumman*]